UNIQUE AUSTRALIAN
ANIMALS

UNIQUE AUSTRALIAN ANIMALS

Illustrator **Rod Scott**

Text by **Margaret Murrant**

LANSDOWNE

For my wife Marie and my
sons Damian and Adrian

CONTENTS

Brush-tailed Possum

Most Australians know this attractive, grey woolly-furred possum. In the bush it makes its nest in the hollow branches of trees, but in towns it sometimes hides in the roofs of houses, coming down at night to feed on buds, fruit and leaves. The size of a cat, it has a pointed snout, long ears and a thick brushy tail which curls and clings so that the possum can hang on to branches.

The female gives birth to a single baby which lives in the pouch.

Sugar Glider

This small gliding possum lives in families in the tree-tops looking for insects and the nectar from blossoms. Like other possums it has hind feet shaped rather like hands, with a clawless big toe which acts like a thumb, giving it a firm grip on branches. It can't fly, but skin stretched between the front and hind legs allows it to glide down like a parachute from one branch to another, its furred tail acting like a rudder to steer it from tree to tree. It has babies in a litter of two, and they live in the pouch for eight weeks.

Fat-tailed Marsupial Mouse or Dunnart

Because it is found in country that is often dry, like the inland of New South Wales and south from Lake Eyre in Central Australia, food is not always plentiful for this little narrow-footed marsupial mouse. Nature has allowed it to develop a special food-storing tail, which swells and looks rather like a carrot when food is plentiful, but which grows very thin when there is not much about. Narrow feet and large ears distinguish this tiny, pointy-toothed animal.

Small insects and living creatures such as grasshoppers, centipedes and lizards are welcome meals for such a fierce little hunter. It nests in fence posts, hollow logs or under tree stumps and rocks, and will stay there sleepily, saving its energy during a drought, so that it does not need so much food.

In times of plenty, the female may produce as many as ten babies in one litter.

Rainbow Lorikeet

The best-known member of the parrot family is the Rainbow Lorikeet. This beautiful bird, named for its brilliant blue, green, orange, yellow and deep violet feathers, is found in forests and woodlands in eastern Australia. It has a special tongue with tiny bristles like a brush which it uses to sweep up nectar from deep inside blossoms. It eats insects and grass as well as stealing fruit and grain from farmers.

Rainbow Lorikeets move in large flocks searching for food and are often tame enough to come into parks and gardens if people stand with dishes and feed them bread soaked with honey.

Koala

The best-known and best-loved of our furred and feathered friends is the Koala. It spends most of its life in the tree-tops where it eats only the leaves of some special, smooth-barked gum trees. A Koala seldom needs to drink water. During the day, it sleeps in the fork of a tree, preferring to move about at night, usually coming down from its tree only to cross over to another.

Every second year, a Koala will have a baby that is just the size of a two-cent piece. Like the Wombat, the mother carries her infant in a backward opening pouch, for about three months. Then it climbs on to its mother's back, where it clings until it is a year old.

Grey Kangaroo

Because he lives in the forests and open woodlands of eastern Australia, the Great Grey Kangaroo is also called the Forester. His short, woolly fur is a soft grey on the body and head, but pales to white on the belly. The female is the same colour, but she is much smaller.

All kangaroos like to rest by day and graze by night, but while the Red Kangaroo prefers to move in large mobs, the Grey is happy in a smaller group of about twenty.

The large thigh muscles of kangaroos enable them to leap in great bounds. The long, strong tail controls their balance.

Red Kangaroo

The mighty male Red Kangaroo stands tall and proud, like a king of the inland plains of Australia. Although he can grow to two metres tall, he is less than the length of your little finger when he is born. He struggles blindly until he reaches his mother's pouch, where he stays drinking her milk until he is about six months old. Called a joey now, he pops his head out of the pouch and nibbles grass when she feeds.

Because the female Red Kangaroo is smaller than the male and a smoky-blue colour, she is often called the Blue Flyer.

During the day kangaroos like to rest beside shady bushes. In the late afternoon, they are to be found drinking at waterholes before moving on at night to graze on herbs and grasses.

Fur Seal

In the past, many of these animals have been killed for their fine, thick fur coats. They breed in rookeries along the southern parts of Australia's coastline, where they gather in hundreds.

The mother seal, or cow, feeds her baby, which is called a pup, on milk, but the adult seals eat fish or shellfish — and sometimes, penguins.

The bull seal and cow are fine swimmers, but they can also bend their hind flippers forward to help them to walk on land.

Fairy Penguin

Like the Emu, the Fairy Penguin cannot fly. But he is a wonderful swimmer, and he can dive and round up a school of small fish to feed his family. He swallows the fish and at the end of a day at sea, he swims home and waddles up the beach to his nesting burrow in the sandhills, using his flippers to balance his fat little body.

With growling noises and flapping his flippers, he coughs up the food for his mate or his chicks, if they are hatched.

Lyrebird

The finest songbird in the Australian bush is the Lyrebird. With his silvery tail displayed, the male bird is very beautiful, so he builds himself a special stage from bare mounds of earth, scattered among the ferns and undergrowth. He decorates these mounds in patterns with bright little objects that he picks up. Then he does his dancing and singing while he displays his splendid tail feathers. As well as his own song, he imitates the calls of many birds, even the Kookaburra. He can also make the sounds of a baby crying, a pack of dogs barking, and a saw felling trees.

The nest-building, hatching the egg and caring for the young are all left to the female. She has one baby chick each year.

Red-tailed Black Cockatoo

Found in heavily timbered country, large flocks of Red-tailed Black Cockatoos feed on the seeds of banksias and eucalypts, and grubs which they dig out of tree trunks.

In Central Australia Aborigines wear the handsome red and black tail-feathers in their hair during corroborees or in rain-dances.

The Cockatoo lays one white egg on a few chips of wood in a nest-hole in the tree.

Sulphur-crested Cockatoo

Also known as the White Cockatoo, this bird has become very popular as a pet. It can sometimes be taught to talk and to wander freely about the house and garden, so that it does not have to be kept in a cage.

The farmer finds it a great pest because it is very fond of his wheat crop. Large flocks fly over and raid the fields, leaving one Cockatoo to stand guard and squawk a warning if danger approaches.

Cockatoos enjoy a long life. Some have been known to live as long as 100 years.

Rob Scott

Echidna

If an Echidna is frightened, it burrows down in soft earth to cling with its strong claws hooked under rocks or roots, or it curls up in a tight ball of sharp spines. Because it protects itself so well, it can hunt in the daytime, probing for termites with its long, sticky tongue.

The mother Echidna develops a special pouch on her body for hatching her single eggs, and holding her baby while it drinks her milk and grows.

It is not a hedgehog, but some people call it a Spiny Anteater.

Platypus

The Platypus is very strange-looking with its duckbill, webbed feet and flattened tail. It swims and dives in streams and lakes for its food, front feet moving like broad, flat paddles, and hind feet and tail steering like a rudder. It closes its eyes and ears to dive and comes to the surface to breathe and chew.

The male platypus can be dangerous when threatened. It has a spur on each back leg which can inflict a poisonous wound.

The female lays two or three soft, rubbery eggs in a grass nest made in its burrow in the mudbank. The mother suckles its young when they hatch.

Kookaburra

Famous throughout the world for its jolly laughter, the Kookaburra belongs only to Australia. It can be heard early in the morning and late in the afternoon calling loudly in a merry family chorus.

It is a member of a bird family called the Kingfishers, but it feeds on lizards and snakes as well as fish, diving on its prey from a lookout perch up in a tree. It has a thick, strong bill, ideal for catching its food.

Some Kookaburras have been tamed enough to visit houses and feed on chopped meat left for them on verandahs. They live in forests as well as in dry country away from water.

Roe Scott

Emu

Australia's biggest bird is one that cannot fly. It is the Emu, a very fast long-distance runner, and a fine swimmer. It is found in groups in most parts of our country's forests and on grassy plains searching for plant foods, grasshoppers and other insects.

The Emu wears its long feathers like a huge swinging cloak above which its finely covered head and neck bob as it walks.

The female lays from five to nine dark-green eggs in a nest made in a hollow in the ground, but then the male takes over. He cares for them and also the downy cream and dark-brown striped chicks when they are born. He scares away the enemies, like the fox, with a loud booming noise like a drum. Foxes like to eat Emu eggs.

Rob Scott

Numbat or Banded Anteater

The numbat is easily recognised by the six white bands which cross the reddish-brown fur of its rump. About the size of a large rat, it has a brushy tail and a pointed snout.

Most pouched animals like to move and hunt at night (nocturnal), but the Numbat can be seen hurrying about in small leaps looking for its food in the daytime. It scratches at termites' nests with its sharp claws and then uses its sticky tongue to flick ants out and into its mouth.

The babies are carried, clinging tightly with claws and mouth, in a very shallow pouch. Found mostly in the dry forests of Western Australia, the Numbat nests in hollow logs and can climb very well.

Designed by Mark Newman

Distributed by National Book Distributors
3/2 Aquatic Drive, Frenchs Forest NSW 2086

Published by Lansdowne Publishing Pty Ltd
Level 5, 70 George Street Sydney NSW 2000, Australia
First published as *Furred and Feathered Friends* 1983
Reprinted in softcover 1995

© Copyright Lansdowne Publishing Pty Ltd 1983
Printed in Hong Kong by South China Printing Co.(Ltd)

National Library of Australia Cataloguing-in-Publication Data

Murrant, Margaret
    Unique australian animals.
    For children.
    ISBN 1 86302 470 0
    1. Zoology – Australia – Juvenile literature.
    I. Scott, Rod.   II. Title.
591.994